The MAILBOX®

grade **Preschool**

S0-BFD-815

Organize JANUARY Now!™

Everything You Need for a Successful January

Monthly Organizing Tools
Manage your time, classroom, and students with monthly organizational tools.

Thematic Idea Collections
Practice essential skills this month with engaging activities and reproducibles.

January in the Classroom
Carry your monthly themes into every corner of the classroom.

Ready-to-Go Learning Centers and Skills Practice
Bring January to life right now!

Managing Editor: Allison E. Ward

Editorial Team: Becky S. Andrews, Kimberley Bruck, Karen P. Shelton, Diane Badden, Thad H. McLaurin, Sharon Murphy, Cindy K. Daoust, Gerri Primak, Karen A. Brudnak, Hope Rodgers, Dorothy C. McKinney, Randi Austin, Janet Boyce, Elizabeth A. Cook, Roxanne LaBell Dearman, Sue Fleischmann, Susan Foulks, Deborah Garmon, Ada Goren, Lucia Kemp Henry, Linda W. Jenks, Carrie Maly, Keely Peasner, Jana Sanderson, Susan Walker

Production Team: Lisa K. Pitts, Pam Crane, Rebecca Saunders, David G. Bullard, Jennifer Tipton Cappoen, Chris Curry, Sarah Foreman, Theresa Lewis Goode, Clint Moore, Greg D. Rieves, Barry Slate, Donna K. Teal, Zane Williard, Tazmen Carlisle, Cat Collins, Marsha Heim, Amy Kirtley-Hill, Lynette Dickerson, Mark Rainey, Angela Kamstra

www.themailbox.com

Manufactured in the United States
10 9 8 7 6 5 4 3 2 1

Table of Contents

Monthly Organizing Tools
A collection of reproducible forms, notes, and other timesavers and organizational tools just for January.

Awards and Brag Tags 4
January Calendar 6
Center Checklist 7
Class List 8
Class Newsletters 9
Clip Art 11
Monthly Planning Form 12
Table and Cubby Tags 13
Open Page 14
Parent Reminder Note 15
School Notes 16
Family Fun 17

Thematic Idea Collections
Fun, child-centered ideas for your favorite January themes.

New Year 18
Friendship 24
Winter 30
Polar Animals 40

January in the Classroom
In a hurry to find a specific type of January activity? It's right here!

Arts & Crafts 50
Bulletin Boards & Displays 56
Centers 60
Circle Time & Games 66
Management Tips 70
Songs, Poems, & Fingerplays 72

Ready-to-Go Learning Centers and Skills Practice
Two center activities you can tear out and use today! Plus a collection of January-themed reproducibles for fine-motor skills practice!

Making a Splash: sorting shapes (Learning Center) 74
Chilly Chums: matching letters (Learning Center) 82
Fine-Motor Fun (Reproducibles) 90

Skills Grid

	New Year	Friendship	Winter	Polar Animals	Centers	Circle Time & Games	Learning Center: Making a Splash	Learning Center: Chilly Chums	Ready-to-Go Skills Practice
Literacy									
letter recognition	19				61	66			
prewriting	20		30						
visual discrimination		24							
cooperative writing		25							
drawing pictures based on stories		26							
story extension			31						
matching letters			32		62			82	
beginning sound /m/			33, 38						
rhyming pictures				40					
positional words				41					
supplying action words				43					
sequencing					60				
Language Development									
follow oral directions				42					
Math									
sorting by colors	18								
visual discrimination	23								
comparing sets		26							
matching colors			31		60				
matching sets to numerals			33						
one-to-one correspondence			39						
counting				40					
matching						66			
sorting shapes							74		
Science									
animal adaptations				42					
Physical Health & Development									
gross-motor skills	20			43		67			
fine-motor skills			32						
tracing									90, 91, 92
cut and glue									93, 94, 95, 96
Creative Arts									
using art media	18								
participate in song	19		30	41					
explore art materials					61				
dramatic play					62				
Social & Emotional Development									
develop friendships		24							
cooperation		25							
social relationships						67			

I'M kicking up my heels over _____ !

student

_____
teacher

_____
date

©The Mailbox® • *Organize January Now!*™ • TEC60969

Who has something "tweet" to tell you?

Me!

©The Mailbox® • *Organize January Now!*™ • TEC60969

BEARING GOOD NEWS!

©The Mailbox® • *Organize January Now!*™ • TEC60969

Awards: Use these awards to reinforce positive behaviors.

Medallion
Tape to a child's clothing or to a crepe paper necklace.

Wristband
Tape the ends together where shown.

Headband
Glue to a construction paper strip sized to fit around a child's head.

Brag tags: Copy the tags on colorful construction paper and use as desired.

January

Sunday	Monday	Tuesday	Wednesday	Thursday	Friday	Saturday

Center Checklist

Name

Center

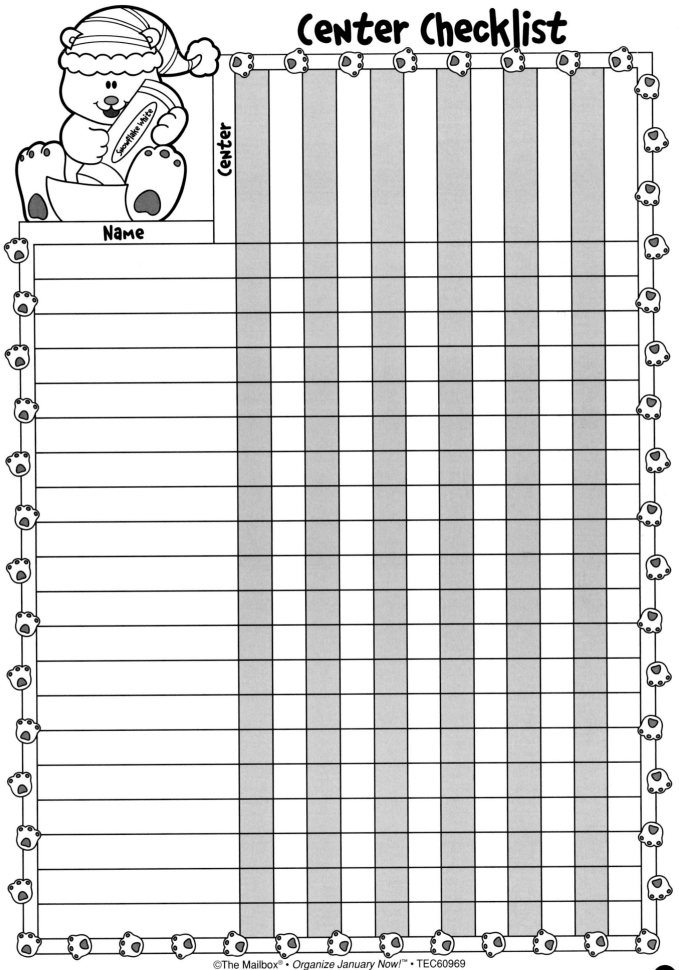

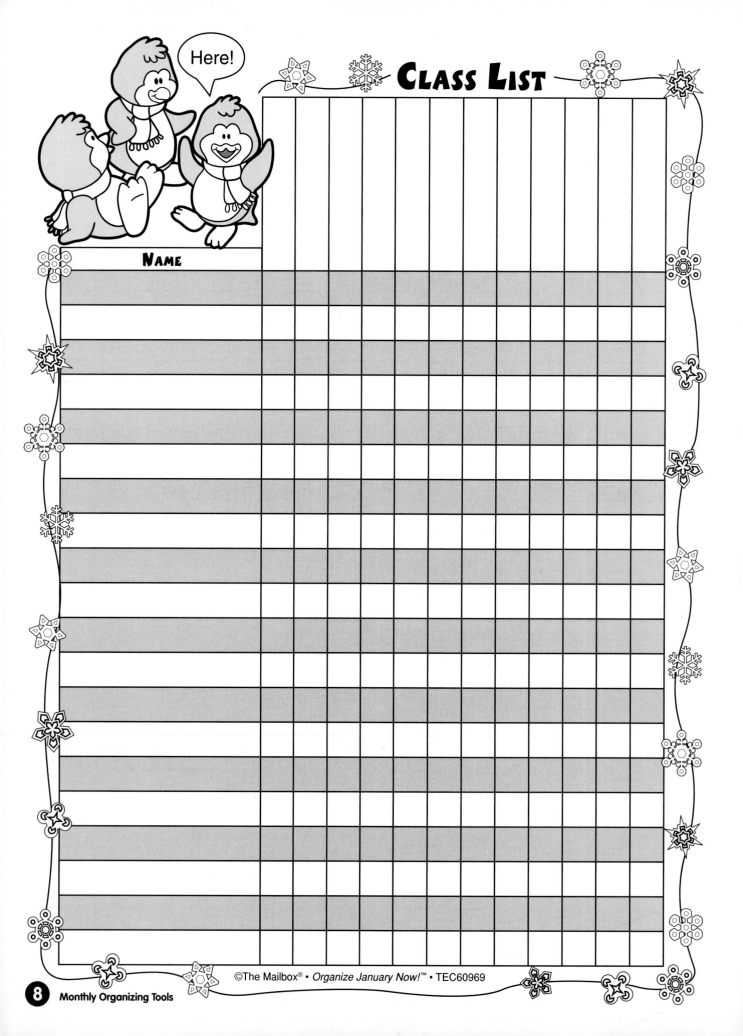

Here!

CLASS LIST

NAME

Classroom News

From _____

Date _____

Special Thanks

Superstars

Look What We Are Learning

Please Remember

Help Wanted

9

Classroom News

Date _____

From _____

New Year!

Happy

TEC60969

TEC60969

Cool News

TEC60969

TEC60969

TEC60969

TEC60969

©The Mailbox® • *Organize January Now!*™ • TEC60969

Clip art: Use the artwork on student papers and on correspondence such as announcements, forms, and parent notes.

Monthly Organizing Tools **11**

Materials to Collect:

Duties This Month:

Meetings:

To Do:

_____

_____

_____

_____

_____

_____

_____

_____

_____

_____

Themes:

Birthdays & Special Dates:

Monthly planning form: Use this handy form to stay on top of January's school-related responsibilities.

TEC60969

TEC60969

TEC60969

©The Mailbox® • *Organize January Now!*™ • TEC60969

Table and cubby tags: Copy these tags on construction paper and personalize them with your youngsters' names. If desired, laminate the tags for durability.

FLAKES

©The Mailbox® • *Organize January Now!*™ • TEC60969

Open: Use this page for parent correspondence or use it with students. For example, ask a child to draw himself dressed in winter clothes. Then have him dictate a sentence about his favorite thing to do on a winter day.

_____
date

Dear Parent,

Please remember

©The Mailbox® • *Organize January Now!*™ • TEC60969

Parent reminder note: Use this note to remind parents of supply requests, field trips, and special events such as classroom parties, school programs, or guest speakers.

Monthly Organizing Tools **15**

SCHOOL NOTE

School Note

School notes: Use these notes for parent communications such as announcing an upcoming event, requesting supplies or volunteers, and writing messages of praise.

Family Fun

Energize a winter day with this snowy family project. Please help your child decorate the snowpal. Use whatever supplies you have on hand, such as crayons, cotton balls, paper or fabric scraps, and glue. Encourage your child to think creatively during the decorating process. We hope to see your completed project by _____.

Sincerely,

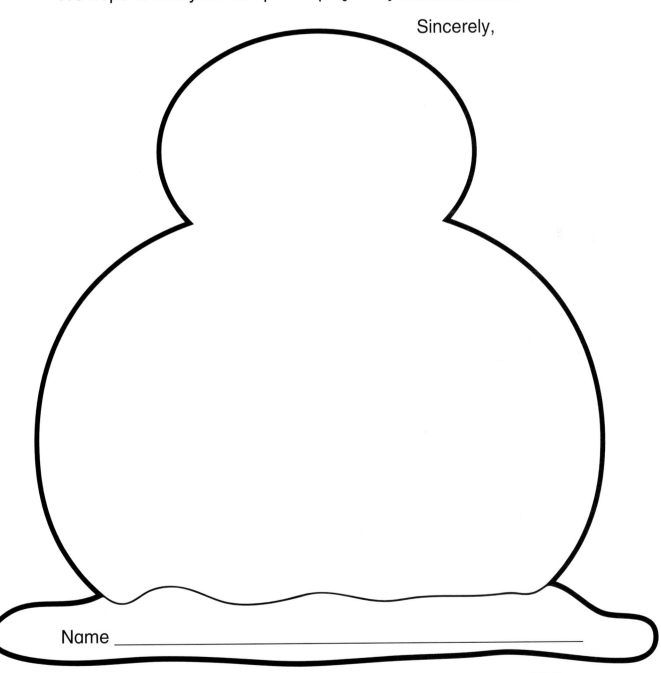

Name _____

Learning Links: develops fine-motor skills, encourages creativity

Note to the teacher: Date and sign a copy of the page. Then make student copies on white construction paper. Write a child's name on a snowpal before sending it home with her. When she returns her project, help her share it with the class. Then cut out her artwork and add it to a display with some quilt batting to represent snow.

New Year

Using art media

Surprise!

The numbers in the new year will appear with a little help from your preschoolers. Squeeze glue onto a sheet of tagboard to form the new year's numbers. Add glue squiggles and dots to resemble confetti and streamers. Allow the glue to dry overnight and then tape the tagboard to a tabletop. Help a child tape a sheet of copy paper over the glue design. Next, have her rub over the paper with the sides of different-colored unwrapped crayons. Surprise! The glue design shows through! Encourage the child to use various colors of crayons for a festive effect. If desired, mount the finished rubbing on a sheet of construction paper.

Sorting by colors

Math

Confetti Celebration

Your youngsters are sure to enjoy tossing some supersize confetti to help celebrate the new year! Cut three different-colored sheets of construction paper into two-inch squares to make confetti. Store the confetti in a bag. Invite a pair of students to a center to toss the confetti in the air while shouting, "Happy New Year!" Then have them gather the scattered confetti and sort it into piles according to color. Once you've checked their work, have the revelers return the confetti to the bag for the next pair.

Count down to the new year with this timely collection of activities!

Letter recognition • • • • • • • • • • • •

Polka-Dot Practice

Make a copy of page 21; then program some of the dots with several familiar alphabet letters. Fill in the remaining dots with symbols. Then give each child in a small group a copy and ask her to lightly color the dots with letters one color and those with symbols another color. For a more challenging activity, help students identify each letter before coloring its dot as you direct.

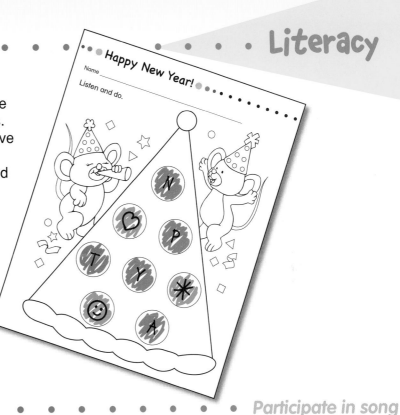

Creative Arts • • • • • • • • • • • • Participate in song

Noisy New Year

Purchase a class supply of noisemakers from a party supply store and give one to each child. Then sing the song shown. Invite each child to play a noisemaker at the end of each line.

(sung to the tune of "If You're Happy and You Know It")

The new year is here, so make some noise!
The new year is here, so make some noise!
Come on girls and boys,
Make some joyful new year noise!
The new year is here, so make some noise!

It's Midnight!

For this midnight movement game, use masking tape to outline a large circle on the floor in an open area. Program index cards with the numbers 1–12; then tape them to the floor inside the circle to resemble a giant clockface. Have students stand around the outside of the clock. Select a movement—such as gallop, hop, tiptoe, walk, or march—and ask students to move around the clock until you shout, "Stop!" Have the child standing closest to the number 12 shout, "It's midnight! Happy New Year!" When the giggles subside, call out a different movement for the next round of play.

New Year's Predictions

Learning to tie shoes, growing taller, or planning a special birthday party—your preschoolers are sure to have some big ideas for the coming year! Give each child a copy of page 22. Write her prediction for the coming year as she dictates for you. Then ask her to illustrate her idea. Bind all the pages to make a class book. If desired, decorate the cover with confetti and glitter glue. Share the resulting book during a group time and place it in your classroom library for continued student enjoyment.

In the new year, I will have a princess birthday party.

Alli

Find a reproducible activity on page 23.

Happy New Year!

Name _____

Listen and do.

Note to the teacher: Use with "Polka-Dot Practice" on page 19.

New Year **21**

In the new year, I will

Note to the teacher: Use with "New Year's Predictions" on page 20.

Party Hat Pairs

Name _____

Color the two hats in each row that match.

Visual Discrimination 23

Friendship

Develop friendships

Rays of Sunshine

Youngsters will display plenty of friendly qualities with this bright, sunny incentive! Post a large sun cutout in an accessible classroom location and store a supply of construction paper rays nearby. Each time a student shows a desired quality, such as sharing a toy or helping a classmate, help him write his name on a ray. Then help him attach it to the sun. When the sun is filled with rays, celebrate your students' friendliness by giving each child a personalized copy of the badge on page 27.

Visual discrimination

Literacy

Picture Pairs

Encourage students to work together at this chummy partner center. To prepare, make two copies of each student's photo. Mount each photo on a colorful card; then write the child's name underneath the photo. Place the cards in a center and have students work together to match each pair. Encourage youngsters to notice both the picture and the written name to make each match. For more advanced students, program one card in each pair with a photo and its corresponding name and the other card with only the name.

Help your preschoolers discover the fabulous fun of friends with these activities!

Be a Friend

Encourage friendly behavior in your classroom with this activity! Invite students to talk about ways to be a friend. Write their responses and names on a chart. When each child has had a turn to share, talk with students about the importance of being a friend to everyone in the class. Then, at the end of the list, write "We promise to be friends." Paint each child's hand with brightly colored paint and have him print it onto the chart. Later, refer to it with great fanfare when your preschoolers demonstrate the recorded actions.

Be a Friend

Friends share.
Jae

Friends are nice.
Emelyn

Friends hug.
Omar

Friends play together.
J'Quon

We promise to be friends.

Sharing Sheet

This project will help little ones see the results of working together—as friends do! Invite each small group, in turn, to take a turn coloring an old sheet with fabric crayons. When the sheet is decorated, set the crayon according to the manufacturer's directions. Share the completed project with youngsters and invite them to notice each other's coloring. Lead students to realize that by working together as friends they were able to create a unique project. Use the completed sharing sheet as an incentive to encourage friendly behavior and cooperation amongst your preschoolers. For example, invite students to sit on their sharing sheet during story times, centers, or anytime a special treat is desired.

A Lot in Common

Your preschoolers discover things that they have in common when they create and compare sets. Seat students in a circle and then give a direction such as "If you like pizza, stand up" or "If you have a sister, stand up." Encourage youngsters to observe the set of students who stand and notice who shares commonalities. Next, ask them to compare the sets using vocabulary such as *more than, fewer than,* and *equal to.* (For more advanced students, you may wish to count the sets to confirm the comparison.) Have everyone sit down before giving the next direction. Continue in this manner for several rounds.

Drawing pictures based on stories • • • • • • • • • • • **Literacy**

Fabulous Friends

For each child, cut out a copy of the booklet cover and pages on pages 27–29. Assemble each booklet and staple it. Explain to youngsters that the pictures in a book go with the words to tell the story. Then, as you slowly read each page aloud, have each child draw himself with a friend to illustrate the text. Reread the completed booklet with student help and then invite youngsters to take their booklets home to share with their families.

I'm a little ray of
sunshine!

_____
name

TEC60969

I'm a little ray of
sunshine!

_____
name

TEC60969

Booklet Cover
Use with "Fabulous Friends" on page 26.

Name _____

Friends share.

1

Friends help each other.

2

Friends work together.

3

Friends play together.

4

Winter

Creative Arts

Winter Dressing

This little ditty is a great reminder for youngsters to bundle up during chilly weather. Place a hat, mittens, a coat, and boots in the middle of your circle. Sing the song as a volunteer points to each item. Later, sing the song with students as they get ready to go outside.

(sung to the tune of "Head, Shoulders, Knees, and Toes")

Hat, mittens, coat, and boots,
Coat and boots.
Hat, mittens, coat, and boots,
Coat and boots.
I am ready to play outside!
Hat, mittens, coat, and boots,
Coat and boots.

Prewriting

Literacy

Snow Creations

Give each child a handful of cotton ball snow to inspire this creative-writing activity. Help each child glue a copy of one of the text strips on page 34 near the bottom of a sheet of light blue construction paper. Read the text strip aloud and encourage youngsters to think of snow-covered objects. Next, ask each child to arrange her snowballs on the paper to make a snow creation. Help her glue the snowballs in place. Then have her dictate to finish the sentence.

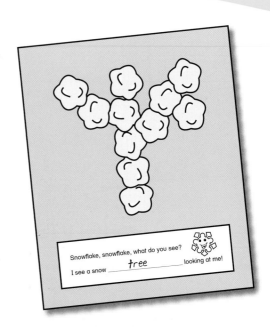

Snowflake, snowflake, what do you see?

I see a snow _tree_ looking at me!

Here's a blizzard of cool ideas to warm up this wintry season!

Snowball Garnish

Share the story *Snowballs* by Lois Ehlert to set the stage for this cool partner activity. After reading, review the illustrations with youngsters and have them name some of the items used to embellish each snow character. Next, place several large snowman cutouts on the floor near the dramatic-play center. Also place at the center dress-up items (such as neckties, scarves, hats, purses, mittens, and vests) and nature items (such as leaves, pinecones, and small twigs). Ask partners to use the items to create their own snow people or pets.

Colorful Snowmen

Frosty friends guide youngsters through this color identification center. Make eight construction paper snowmen from the pattern on page 35 and color each hat a different color. Cut three colored construction paper circles (buttons) to match each hat. Store the buttons and snowmen in a bag. Invite a student to choose a snowman and lay it flat on a table. Have him name the color of its hat and then decorate the snowman with matching colored buttons. Encourage him to repeat the process with each remaining snowman.

Two to a Sled

Color several construction paper copies of the dog and sled patterns on page 36. Program each set with matching letters and then cut them apart. Detach the flap from an equal number of business-size envelopes. Next, glue each sled onto an envelope. Attach the sleds to a wall or bulletin board within children's reach. Store the dog cards nearby. Then invite a youngster to match sets of letters by placing each dog in the corresponding sled.

Fine-motor skills ·

Physical Health & Development

Lacy Snowflakes

Expect a blizzard of unique snowflakes with this lacing activity. Punch holes around a tagboard copy of the snowflake pattern on page 68 for each child. Knot one end of a 36" length of white yarn, wrap the other end with tape, and thread the taped end through one hole. Have a child lace the yarn through each hole on the snowflake. Then help her decorate the snowflake with glitter glue.

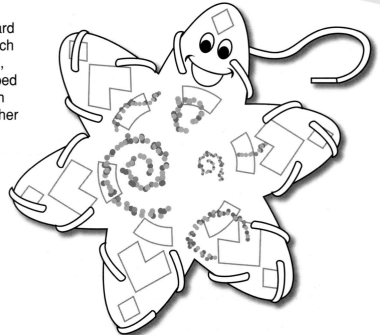

Slumbering Bears

Count on these sleepy bears to help youngsters practice matching sets. Make five copies of page 37; then color and cut out the patterns. Program each cave with a different number from 1 to 5. Store the bears in a basket. Give each of five youngsters a cave. Help each child name her cave's number and then place the corresponding number of bears on it. Have youngsters return their bears to the basket, trade caves, and repeat the activity.

Literacy • • • • • • • • • • • *Beginning sound /m/*

M Is for *Mitten*

Your little snow shovelers will dig this small-group sound-matching activity! Fill your sand table or a large plastic tub with white packing peanuts (snow). Next, bury in the snow several items whose names begin with *m,* such as a mitten, a toy mouse, and a stuffed monkey. Also bury some items whose names do not begin with *m.* Show your group several objects that begin with the /m/ sound and ask them to repeat the sound. Then have one child use a toy shovel to dig through the snow until he finds an object. Ask him to show the object to the group, name it, and tell if its name begins with /m/ or not. Then have him rebury the object. Repeat the process until each child has had a turn.

Find reproducible activities on pages 38–39.

Snowflake, snowflake, what do you see?

I see a snow _____ looking at me!

Snowflake, snowflake, what do you see?

I see a snow _____ looking at me!

Snowflake, snowflake, what do you see?

I see a snow _____ looking at me!

Use with “Colorful Snowmen” on page 31.

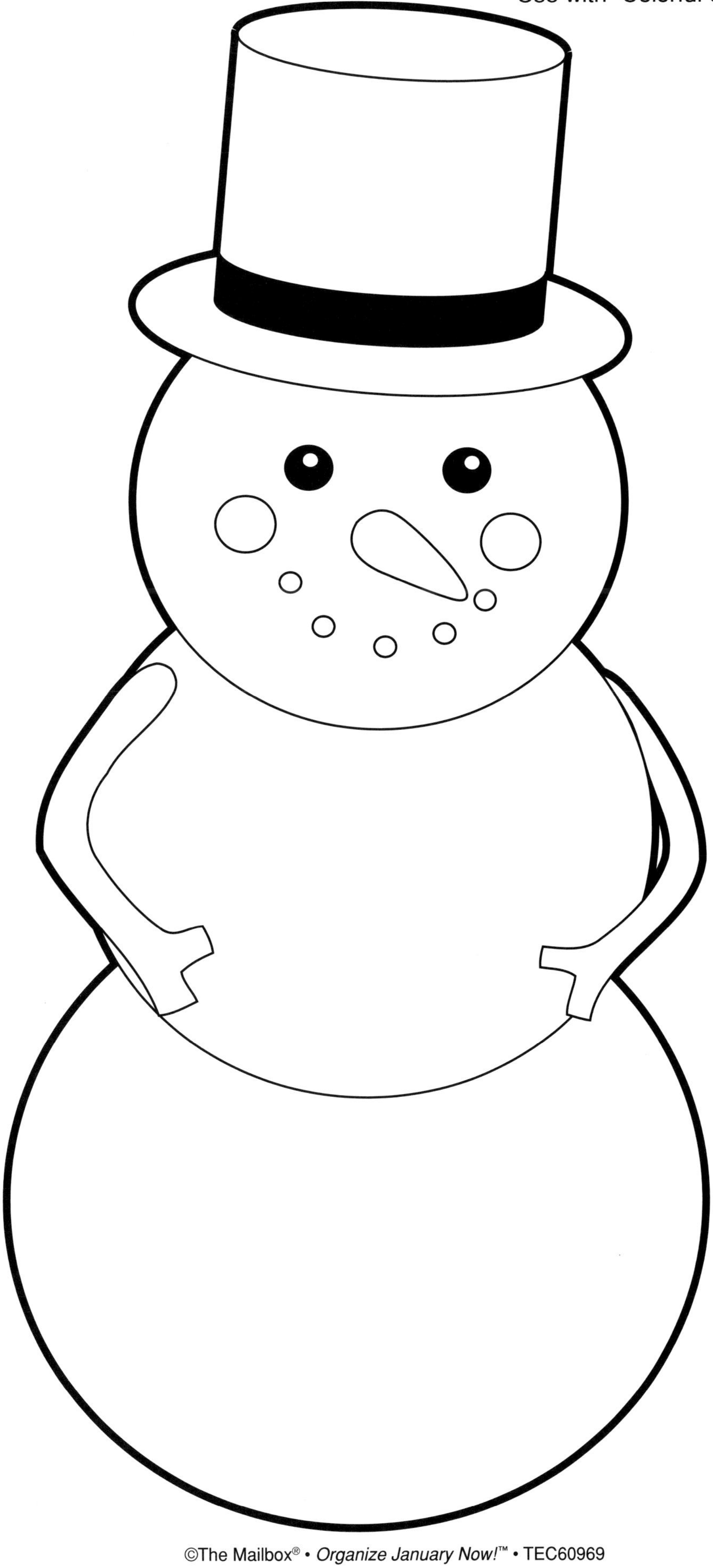

Dog and Sled Patterns

Use with "Two to a Sled" on page 32.

TEC60969

TEC60969

TEC60969

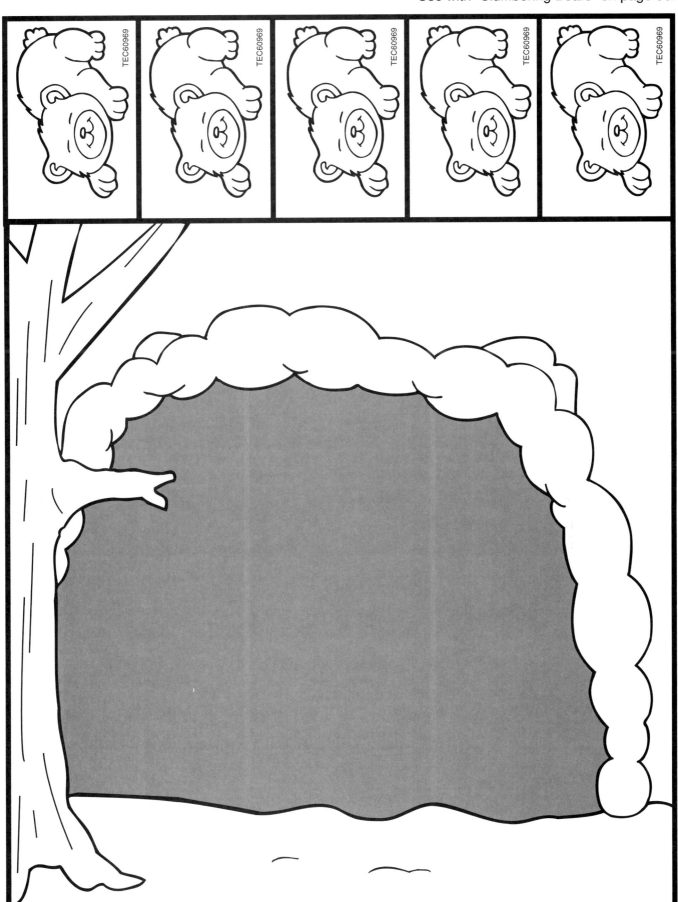

M Is for Mittens

Name _____

🖍 Color.

✂ Cut.

🧴 Glue the pictures that begin like 🧤.

Beginning Sound /m/

Snow Toppers

Name _____

✂ Cut. Match. 🧴 Glue.

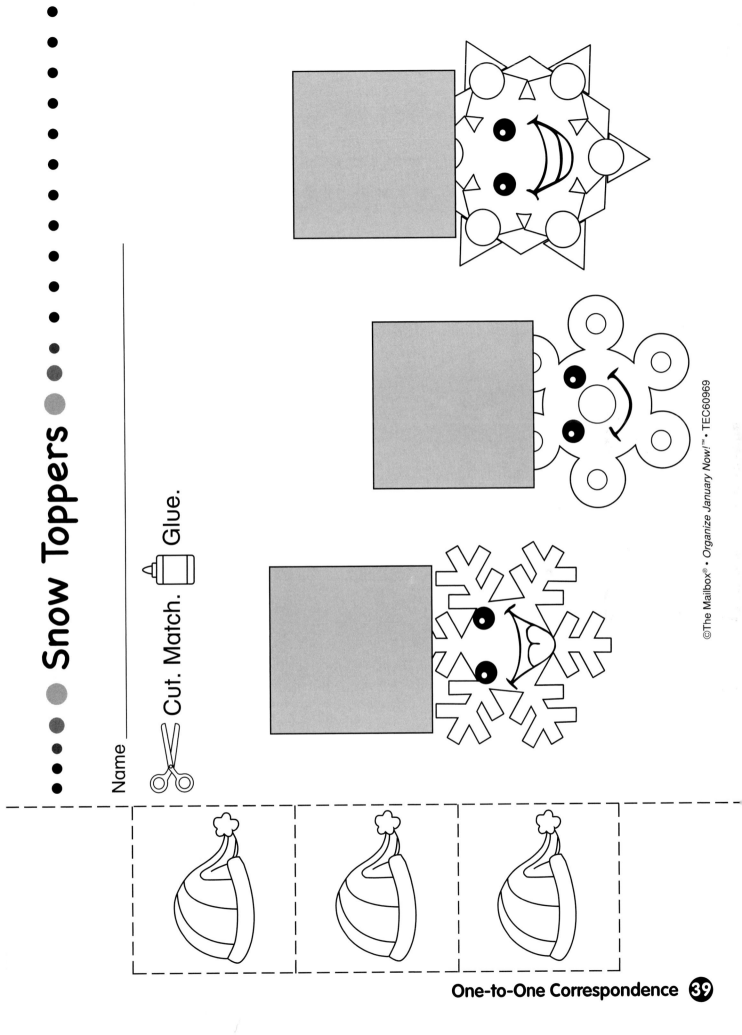

©The Mailbox® • *Organize January Now!*™ • TEC60969

One-to-One Correspondence 39

Polar Animals

Ice Is Nice

Floating icebergs make rhyming practice fun! Color and cut out a copy of the rhyming picture cards on page 44. Use clear packing tape to attach each rhyming pair to a different foam plate. Puzzle-cut each plate into two pieces and place them in your water table to resemble ice pieces. A child chooses an ice piece and names the picture. Then he finds the ice piece with the rhyming picture and puts the pieces together to create an iceberg. He continues in this manner with the remaining pieces of ice.

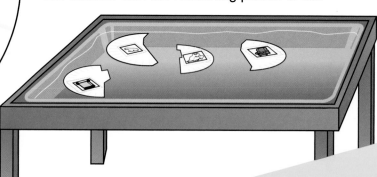

Penguin Place

You'll find penguins aplenty in this partner game! Cut apart two copies of the game cards on page 45; then stack the cards facedown. Use markers to color eight wooden ice-cream spoons to resemble penguins as shown. Give each child four penguins and a slab of white play dough (iceberg). To play, a child draws a card. If the card shows standing penguins, he counts them and inserts the corresponding number of his penguins into his iceberg. If the card shows a diving penguin, he removes one penguin from his iceberg and places it to the side. (If he has an empty iceberg, he does nothing.) Then he places the card under the stack. Partners continue in this manner until each child has four penguins on his iceberg.

Little ones are sure to have frosty fun with this
cool collection of polar animal ideas.

Participate in song

Cool Moms

How do polar animal mothers love their babies?
Youngsters find out when they sing this warm tune!

(sung to the tune of "The Wheels on the Bus")

A mama [puffin] loves with her [wings],
With her [wings],
With her [wings].
A mama [puffin] loves with her [wings],
All through the day.

*Repeat the song, replacing the underlined word pairs
for each additional verse.*
seal, flippers
polar bear, paws
Arctic fox, nose

Literacy

Positional words

Where Is Little Seal?

Reinforce language skills as youngsters help a
little seal swim through the pages of this booklet.
Cut out a copy of pages 46–48 and the seal pattern
on page 44 for each child. Staple the booklet pages
together in order. Next, tape one end of an eight-
inch length of yarn onto the back of the booklet and
the other end onto the back of the seal as shown.
Give each child in a small group a booklet. As you
read the text aloud, guide little ones to place the
seal in the correct position on each booklet page.
Then invite each child to color his booklet and take
it home to share with his family.

Little Seal is **beside.**

Follow oral directions

Home, Sweet Home

Youngsters get in step with polar animals during this whole-group game. On a classroom wall, display a polar bear cutout to represent the North Pole. Mount a penguin cutout on the opposite wall to represent the South Pole. (If desired, enlarge the patterns on pages 45 and 49.)

To begin, tell students that polar bears live near the North Pole and penguins live near the South Pole. You may wish to show youngsters the North and South Poles on a globe. Divide students into two groups: polar bears and penguins. Arrange the groups back-to-back in the middle of an open area, with the polar bears facing the North Pole and the penguins facing the South Pole. Designate a finish line for each group and explain that the polar bears are traveling home to the North Pole and the penguins are traveling home to the South Pole. Next, call out directions for each group, such as "Polar bears hop twice north" or "Penguins waddle three times south." Continue until each group has reached its home at the North or South Pole finish line.

Animal adaptations

Science

Polar Pal

This cool activity shows youngsters how a polar bear stays warm in the frozen Arctic. Explain that underneath all that white fur, polar bears have black skin that holds the sun's warmth. Then give each child a black construction paper bear cutout (pattern on page 45), a sheet of blue construction paper, and a handful of thick white yarn pieces (fur). Ask youngsters to name the color of a polar bear's fur; then share that white fur helps hide the bear in snow and ice. Have each child glue the fur onto her polar bear. Next, have her use a white crayon to draw snow and ice on her blue paper. Then have her glue her polar bear onto its snowy home.

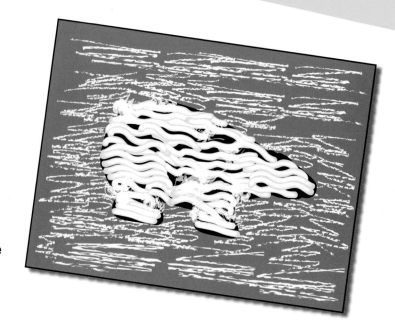

Plenty of Penguins

A penguin waddles, climbs, and slides! Guide youngsters to consider the different ways penguins move as they help make this chilly display. Invite youngsters to pretend to be penguins moving about. Then ask each child to name one way a penguin moves. Record each child's response on a cutout copy of the penguin pattern on page 49. Have him illustrate his idea in the space provided and then color his penguin as desired. Mount the completed penguins on a large iceberg cutout.

Penguins waddle.

Bear Paws

Your little cubs will enjoy swimming through this cool game! Choose two students to pretend to be polar bears and pull white socks over their hands for paws. Have the polar bears join hands above their heads to form an arch. Sing the song shown as the other children pretend to be polar bear cubs swimming under the arch. When the polar bears hear "Polar bear paws!" they lower their hands to trap a cub. The bears gently swing the cub back and forth, releasing him at the end of the song. Then choose another pair of polar bears and repeat the activity.

(sung to the tune of "London Bridge")

Little cubs are swimming about,
Swimming about, swimming about.
Little cubs are swimming about.
Polar bear paws!

Take a cub and play with him,
Play with him, play with him.
Take a cub and play with him.
Polar bear paws!

Rhyming Picture Cards

Use with "Ice Is Nice" on page 40.

Seal Pattern

Use with "Where Is Little Seal?" on page 41.

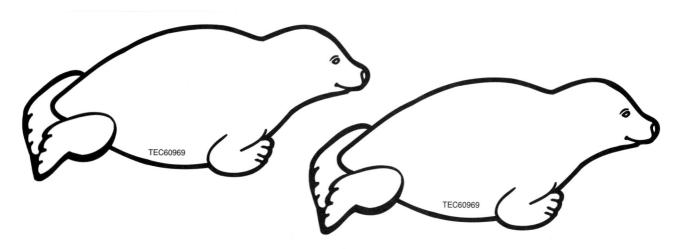

©The Mailbox® • *Organize January Now!*™ • TEC60969

Polar Bear Pattern

Use with "Polar Pal" on page 42.

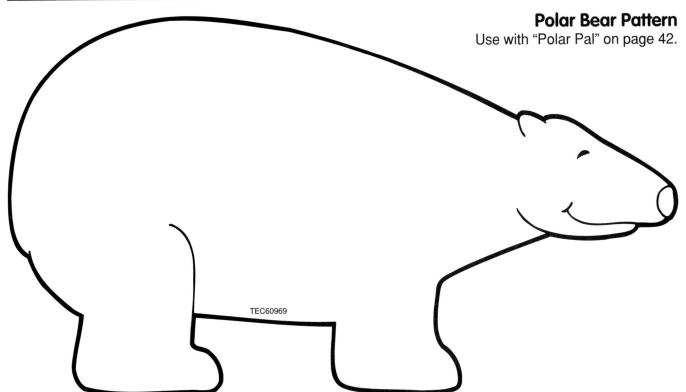

Where Is Little Seal?

Name _____

©The Mailbox® • *Organize January Now!*™ • TEC60969

Little Seal is **over.**

1

Little Seal is **under.**

2

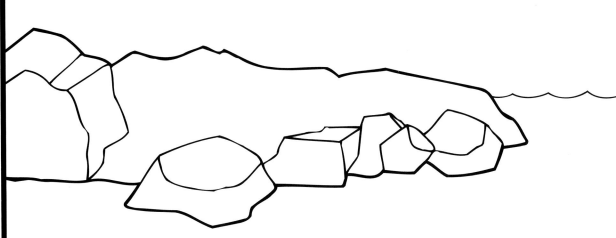

Little Seal is **on.**

3

Little Seal is **beside.**

4

Little Seal is **between.**

5

Penguins

TEC60969

Countdown Collage

To make a festive New Year's Day collage, brush thinned white glue over a sheet of black construction paper. Press a flattened foil cupcake liner (or use a circle cut from aluminum foil) onto the wet glue to make a disco ball. Then add shredded gift bag filler and colorful glitter. Finally, toss some colorful confetti onto the collage and set it aside to dry.

Supersize Snowpal

Use white tempera paint to outline a snowperson on a two-foot length of waxed paper for each child. To make a snowpal, fingerpaint with white tempera to fill the outline. For a glistening finish, sprinkle on sugar. Once the paint is dry, add sticky-dots for eyes and a mouth and glue on a precut carrot nose, a crepe paper scarf, and other construction paper details. Then display these snowpals in a window, where the translucent waxed paper will give them a winter glow.

It's an Igloo!

In advance, snip one-inch strips of white copy paper to represent ice blocks. Then, to make an igloo, glue rows of ice blocks on a light blue construction paper copy of page 54. Trim some of the squares to fit inside the rounded edges. Glue small white paper scraps to the sky above the igloo to resemble snowflakes. Finish the project by gluing stretched cotton ball "snow" across the bottom of the paper.

Welcome!

Waddling Penguin

To make a penguin, trace around a child's shoe on black paper and cut out the shape. Have a child paint a white oval (tummy) on the large part of her cutout. When the paint is dry, she adds two paper hole reinforcements for eyes and glues on an orange paper triangle for a beak. To give the penguin a waddle, fold half a paper plate in half; then glue it to the back of the penguin as shown. Unfold the paper plate half until the penguin can balance upright and rock back and forth.

Fuzzy Polar Bear

To make a bear, fold a 9" x 12" sheet of white construction paper in half. Tear off both corners from the folded edge; then tear a semicircle from both thicknesses of the open edge as shown. Glue a white construction paper bear head (pattern on page 55) to the folded edge of the paper. Use a black marker to add toes to the two front feet. Then brush the front of the bear with slightly diluted white glue. Glue stretched cotton balls all over the bear, avoiding only the face. Finally, glue on a cotton ball tail. Unfold the paper slightly to make the bear stand on a tabletop.

Wintry Whirligig

Hang these projects from your classroom ceiling to give your room the feel of a winter wonderland! To make one, use an empty thread spool dipped in light blue tempera paint to make prints on two thin white paper plates. While the paint is wet, sprinkle the plates with silver glitter and shake off the excess. When the paint is dry, tape a few lengths of iridescent, silver, or white curling ribbon to the back of one plate; then glue the two plates together back-to-back. Add a ribbon loop to the top of the whirligig for hanging.

Fabulous Foil Flakes

These shiny snowflakes have something in common with real ones—each one will be unique! To make one, draw three lines to outline a simple snowflake on a sheet of construction paper. Tear a small piece of aluminum foil and glue it to the intersection of the lines. Then tear more pieces of foil and glue them along the lines until a desired effect is achieved. When the glue is dry, mount the snowflake on a larger frame of another color of construction paper.

Ice Castle

To make an ice castle, dip a small square sponge into white tempera paint and then make prints on a 12" x 18" sheet of dark construction paper. "Build" the castle with the squares; then top the turrets with prints from a small triangular sponge. While the paint is still wet, sprinkle the castle with salt or iridescent glitter. Once the paint is dry, glue a personalized door cutout (pattern on page 55) on the castle.

Welcome
to
Kiley 's
Ice Castle

Welcome!

Note to the teacher: Use with "It's an Igloo!" on page 51.

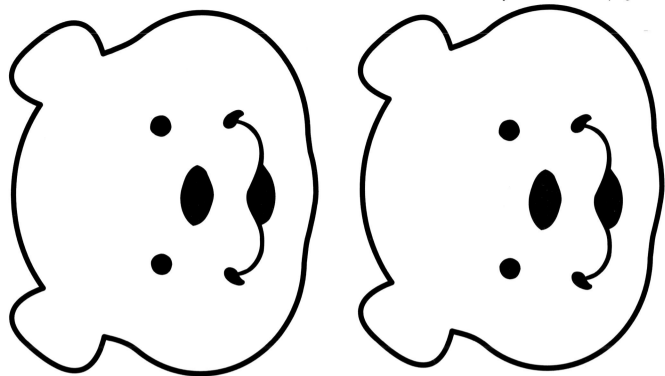

Castle Door Pattern
Use with "Ice Castle" on page 53.

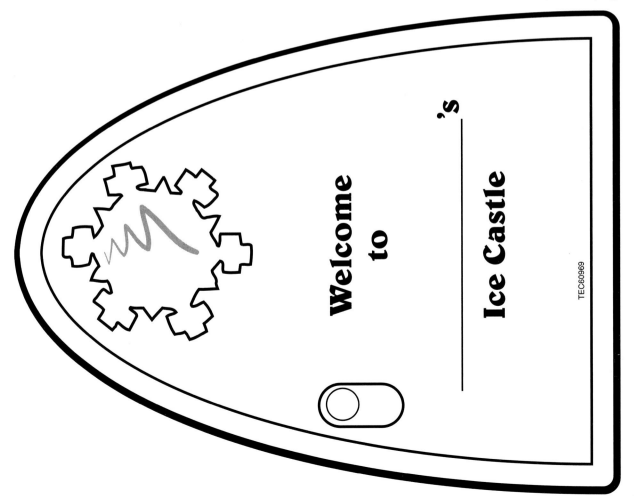

Welcome to

's

Ice Castle

TEC60969

Bulletin Boards &

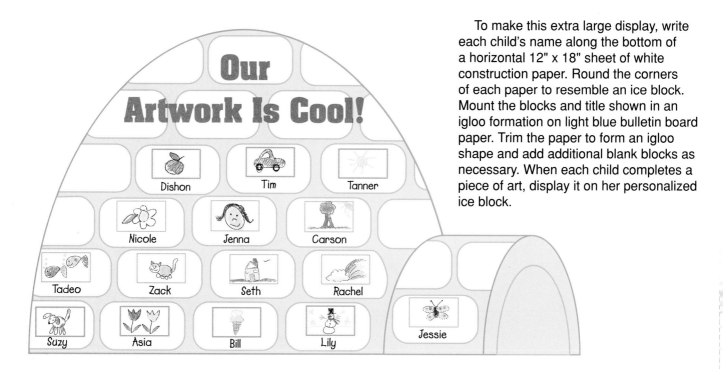

To make this extra large display, write each child's name along the bottom of a horizontal 12" x 18" sheet of white construction paper. Round the corners of each paper to resemble an ice block. Mount the blocks and title shown in an igloo formation on light blue bulletin board paper. Trim the paper to form an igloo shape and add additional blank blocks as necessary. When each child completes a piece of art, display it on her personalized ice block.

To make a multisensory polar bear, have each child paint a tagboard polar bear cutout (pattern on page 58) with thinned white glue. Then have him cover the bear with uncooked oatmeal. After the glue dries, help him shake off the excess oatmeal and use a black permanent marker to draw facial features. Display these playful pals on a bulletin board along with white paper snowdrifts and the title shown.

Displays

On a length of dark blue bulletin board paper, post the title shown. Paint each child's palm and fingers with white tempera paint. Have each youngster press her hand onto the paper to resemble a falling snowflake. Then use a white pencil or crayon to write each child's name under the resulting print.

Give each child a personalized construction paper mug cutout (pattern on page 59). Have him color the top of the mug brown and decorate the rest of the mug using various craft supplies such as bingo daubers, glitter, ribbon scraps, or markers. Then invite him to top the mug with white construction paper squares to resemble marshmallows. Cover a board with a tablecloth and mount the mugs and the title shown.

TEC60969

©The Mailbox® • *Organize January Now!*™ • TEC60969

Use with "Warm and Cozy in Ms. Cook's Room!" on page 57.

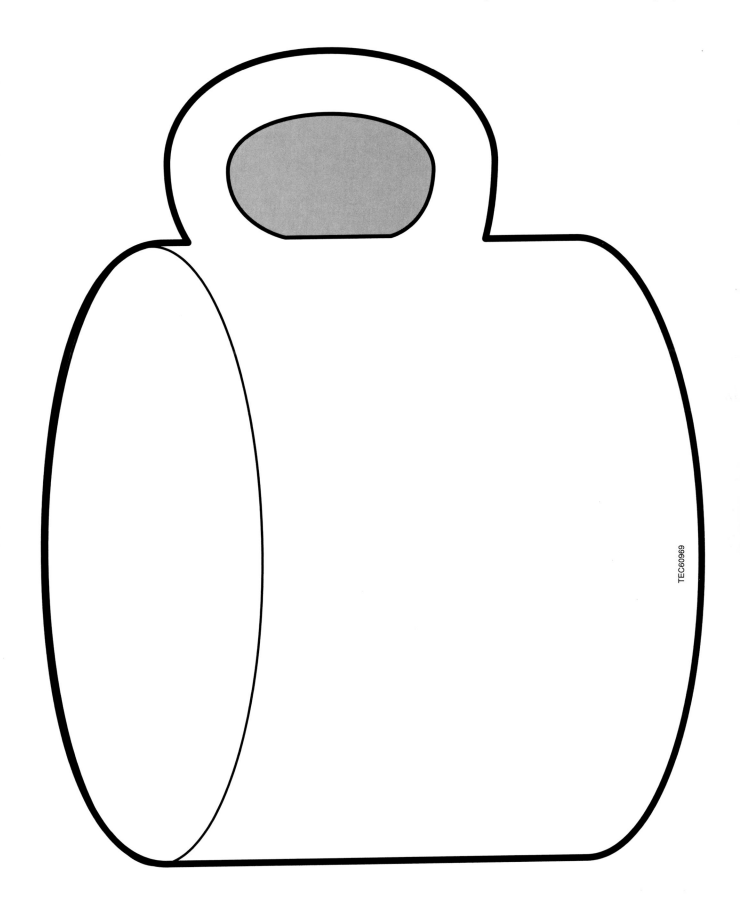

TEC60969

Centers

Math

Matching colors

Mitten Match

Dress up your math center with some toasty warm mittens in a rainbow of colors! Duplicate the mitten pair pattern on page 63 on several different colors of construction paper. Cut out the mittens; then place them in a basket at your math center. A child matches each pair by color.

Sequencing

Literacy

Bundle Up!

Outfit your literacy center to inspire interest in winter clothes. Place a class supply of page 64 at a center along with 4" x 18" paper strips, crayons, scissors, and glue. A child colors a copy of the cards and then cuts them apart. Then he glues the cards in sequential order on a paper strip. For an added challenge, ask each child to describe the actions pictured on the cards.

Letter recognition

Alphabet Soup

Winter is the perfect time for a hot bowl of soup, so stir some up in your sensory tub! Partially fill the tub with water and float some craft foam letters (noodles) and shapes (vegetables) in the water. Provide spoons, ladles, and some large unbreakable bowls. A child in this center serves himself some soup. Then he spoons the veggies back into the tub, leaving behind the letters. Challenge more advanced students to name each letter in their bowls.

Creative Arts

Explore art materials

Icy Painting

Here's an art exploration that doubles as a simple science experiment! To prepare, freeze a few small plastic containers of water that have each been tinted with a different color of food coloring. Have each child in your art center brush a paintbrush on a block of ice and then paint onto a sheet of paper. Youngsters will quickly tell you that there's nothing on their brushes! Next, give each child a chance to sprinkle some salt over the blocks of ice. Have little ones observe for a few minutes as the salt begins to melt the ice. After the salt has had time to do its work, have youngsters dip their brushes again and paint with these very cool watercolors!

Creative Arts

Hot Chocolate Shop

Transform your dramatic-play area into a hot chocolate shop! To make the shop, set up a table and chairs, menus, napkins, foam cups, a plastic measuring cup, and aprons, pads, and pencils. Fill a large pot with brown shredded paper and a small container with cotton balls.

A child pretends to be a server, takes a customer's order, and then uses the measuring cup to put paper shreds (hot chocolate) into a foam cup for a customer. Then he tops it with a cotton ball (marshmallow). In no time at all, you'll have servers taking orders and serving delicious hot chocolate to lots of customers!

Matching letters

Literacy

It's Snowing

To prepare for this frosty center, cut out a few construction paper copies of the center mat on page 65. Program each mat with a different letter in each circle, taking care to make each mat different. Place the mats at a center along with a stack of alphabet cards and a supply of cotton balls or white pom-poms (snowballs).

To play, a child chooses a center mat. She draws an alphabet card from the stack and checks her mat for the identical letter. If she has it, she covers the letter with a snowball. If she does not, she places the card under the stack and draws another. She continues in this manner until she has covered all the letters on her mat. If time allows, she repeats the activity with a new center mat.

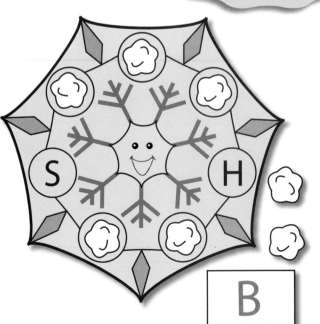

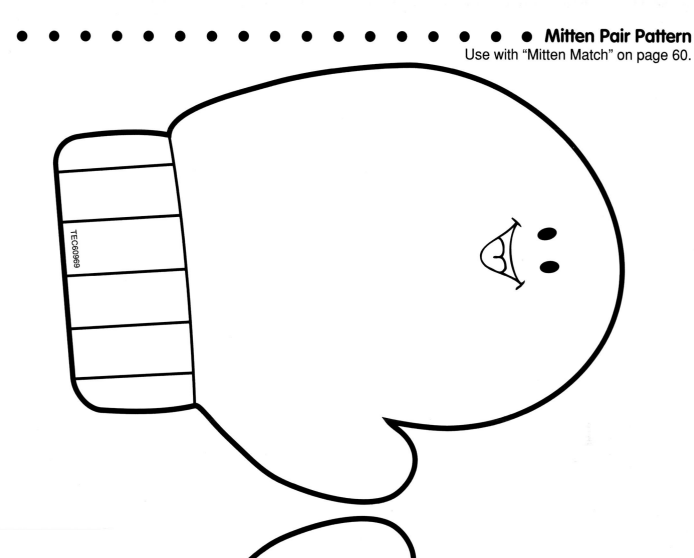

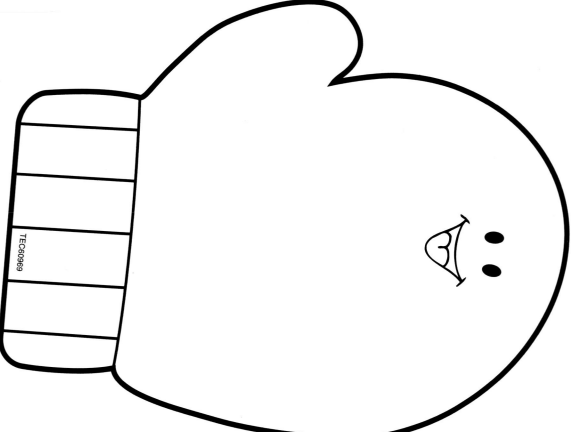

TEC60969

TEC60969

TEC60969

TEC60969

TEC60969

Mitten Buddies

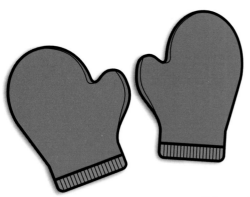

To prepare for this toasty warm game, gather enough pairs of mittens so that you have one mitten for each child in your class (or use the patterns on page 63 to make construction paper mittens). Invite each child to choose a mitten to wear. Then, at your signal, have youngsters search for the child wearing the matching mitten. Direct the matching pair to give each other a mitten high five. Then have each student trade her mitten with a classmate other than her partner and wait for your signal to repeat the activity.

Letter recognition

Literacy

Snowball Stop!

Here's a cool version of the traditional hot potato game. Make a set of cards that includes a variety of letters and a few extra numbers and shapes. Have youngsters pass a foam ball (snowball) around the circle. After a few moments call, "Snowball stop!" Then display a card. Ask the child holding the snowball if the card shows a letter. If he agrees that it does, help him identify the letter. If it does not show a letter, he says, "Brrr," as he shivers. Then he passes the snowball to begin the next round.

Gross-motor skills

Physical Health & Development

Snowflake Dance

There'll be a whole lot of movin' going on when youngsters make these snowflakes! Help each child tape a white crepe paper streamer onto a snowflake cutout (pattern on page 68). Play some music and have each youngster hold a snowflake. Guide the group to move their snowflakes to match the rhythm of the music. End the activity by inviting little ones to slowly flutter their snowflakes to the floor as they sit down.

Social & Emotional Development

Social relationships

Fair or Unfair?

Preschoolers express an understanding of fairness with this puppet activity. Copy, cut apart, and fold a class supply of the puppet patterns on page 69. Tape a craft stick handle inside each one; then tape the bottom and sides of the puppet together. Describe several different fair and unfair situations, such as the ones shown. Have each child show the smiling face puppet if she thinks the situation is fair. Or, if she thinks the situation is unfair, have her show the frowning face puppet.

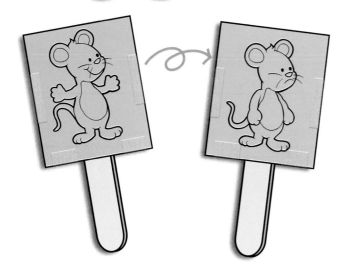

- Two children are in the sandbox. One has two sand pails and the other has none.
- Two friends are sharing a cookie.
- Some girls are inside their playhouse. A boy is outside, and there is a sign that says "No boys allowed."
- A child offers a toy truck to his friend and says, "You can have a turn now."

Snowflake Pattern
Use with "Lacy Snowflakes" on page 32 and "Snowflake Dance" on page 67.

TEC60969

TEC60969

TEC60969

TEC60969

TEC60969

Management Tips

Winter Gear Clip

Help youngsters keep their winter clothing neat and tidy with these personalized clips. Cut out a large poster board snow boot and label it as shown. Personalize a spring-type clothespin for each child and clip them around the cutout. Attach the cutout to a wall near the coat area. When youngsters arrive, help each child find his clothespin and clip his boots together. If desired, also make a mitten cutout with personalized clothespins for youngsters to clip mittens onto coats.

Motivational Snowman

Getting this cool snowman dressed inspires little ones' good behavior. Display one small and one large white paper plate in a snowman formation. Add eyes and a mouth. Color and cut out a copy of the patterns on page 71. Store the patterns near the snowman. Tell youngsters that the class will need to work together to dress the snowman. Then, every time you notice the class exhibiting outstanding behavior, add a new piece to the snowman.

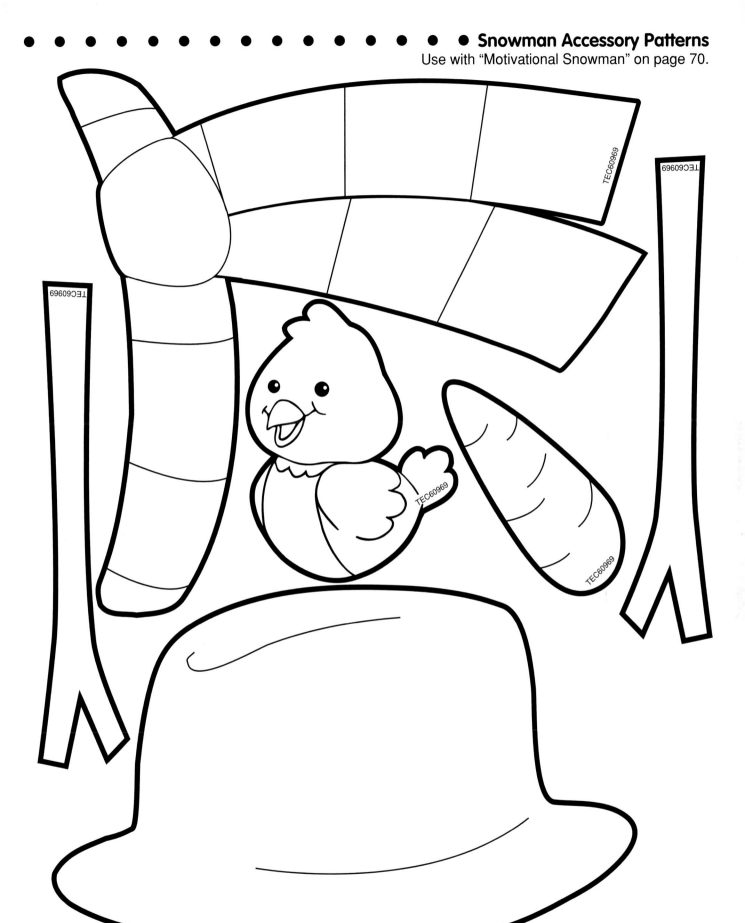

Twist and Pop!

Here's a snappy New Year's tune that's perfect for fine-motor practice! Ask each youngster to hold a rolled-up piece of bubble wrap quietly as you sing the song. Then have him twist and pop the bubble wrap roll to celebrate the new year.

(sung to the tune of "Are You Sleeping?")

It's a new year!
It's a new year!
Did you hear?
Did you hear?
Gone is December.
Christmas we'll remember.
Jump and cheer!
A new year!

Penguin Parade

Pretending to be a penguin makes this action poem fun!

Here come the penguins,
Marching straight and tall.
Watch them waddle;
They never fall!

Put hands down at sides.
March in place.
Waddle back and forth.
Waddle.

See their webbed feet,
Sliding on the snow.
With black and white feathers,
They're warm when cold winds blow!

Walk with feet pointed outward.
Pretend to slide on snow.
Hug self.
Puff cheeks and blow.

Fingerplays

Winter Wonder

Celebrate the winter season with this cool song.

(sung to the tune of "Do Your Ears Hang Low?")

Is it winter now?
Did some snow fall on the ground?
Are fluffy snowflakes swirling,
And twirling all around?
Can you build a big snowman
Before your neighbor can?
It is winter now!

Fond Friendships

Promote classmate friendships with this sweet poem.

It's nice to have friends;
They help in many ways.
If you're feeling sad,
Friends brighten up your day.

Be kind to everyone,
And they'll be kind to you.
When you are a good friend,
You'll have lots of friends too.

Making a Splash

A ready-to-use center mat and cards

Materials:

center mat to the right
center cards on pages 77 and 79
resealable plastic bag

Preparing the center:

Cut out the cards and put them in the bag.

Using the center:

1. A child removes the cards from the bag and lays them shape side up in the center area.
2. He sorts the cards onto the mat by matching the shapes.
3. To check his work, he turns over each stack of cards. If each card in the stack has the same picture on the back, his work is complete. If not, he turns the cards over and rearranges them until they are sorted correctly.

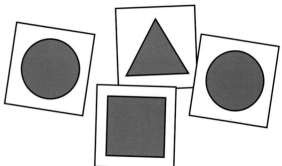

Family Follow-Up

After a youngster completes the center activity, have him take home a copy of page 81 to complete with a parent.

74 Making a Splash

Making a Splash

Sort.

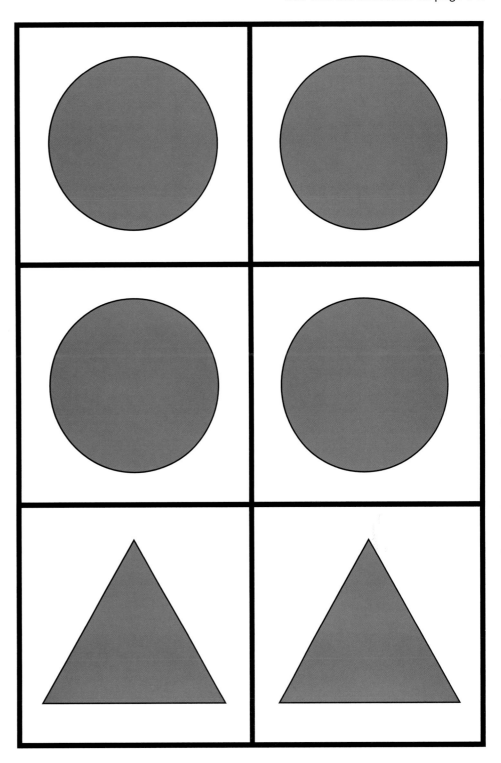

Making a Splash
TEC60969

Making a Splash
TEC60969

Making a Splash
TEC60969

Making a Splash
TEC60969

Making a Splash
TEC60969

Making a Splash
TEC60969

Making a Splash
TEC60969

Making a Splash
TEC60969

Making a Splash
TEC60969

Making a Splash
TEC60969

Making a Splash
TEC60969

Making a Splash
TEC60969

Dear Parent,
   We have been sorting by shape. Please point to each shape and ask your child to show you a matching shape.

Chilly Chums

A ready-to-use center mat and cards

Materials:
center mat to the right
letter cards on pages 85 and 87
resealable plastic bag

Preparing the center:
Cut out the cards and put them in the bag.

Using the center:
1. A child removes the cards from the bag and places each one letter side up in the center area.
2. She chooses a card and then finds its match.
3. She turns the cards over to check her answer. If the pictures on the backs of the cards match, she places the cards on the mat. If not, she searches for the correct card to make a matching pair. When she finds the card, she places both cards on the mat.
4. She repeats Steps 2 and 3 until all the cards are placed on the mat.

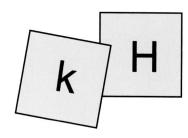

Family Follow-Up
After a youngster completes the center activity, have her take home a copy of page 89 to complete with a parent.

Chilly Chums

Match.

N	N
b	b
H	H

Chilly Chums
TEC60969

Chilly Chums
TEC60969

Chilly Chums
TEC60969

Chilly Chums
TEC60969

Chilly Chums
TEC60969

Chilly Chums
TEC60969

k	k
D	D
†	†

Chilly Chums **87**

Chilly Chums
TEC60969

Chilly Chums
TEC60969

Chilly Chums
TEC60969

Chilly Chums
TEC60969

Chilly Chums
TEC60969

Chilly Chums
TEC60969

Dear Parent,
   We have been matching letters. Help your child draw a line from each letter on the left to its match on the right.

W

r

G

e

r

W

e

G

Mice on Ice

Name _____

Trace.

Tracing

Bear's Balloons

Name _____

Trace.

Color.

Smiling Snowpals

Name _____

Trace.

Color.

Tracing

A Fabulous Flake!

Color.

Cut.

Glue.

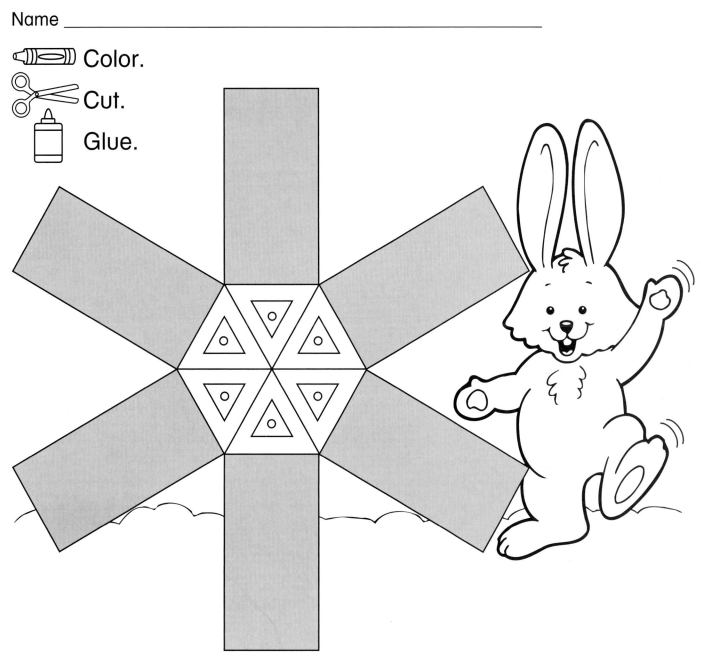

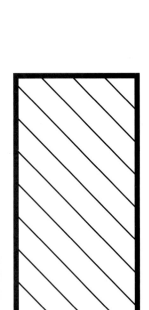

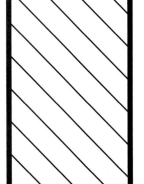

Supersize Scarf

Name _____

Color.

Cut.

Glue.

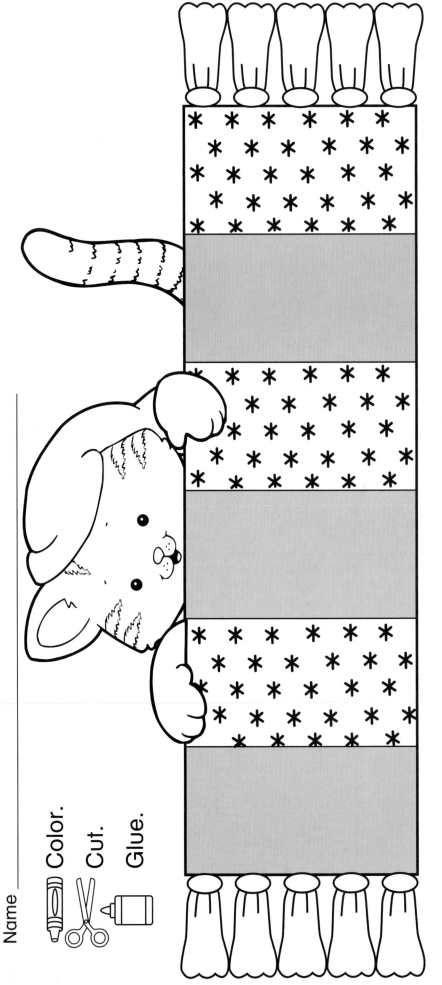

Cut and Glue

It's Midnight!

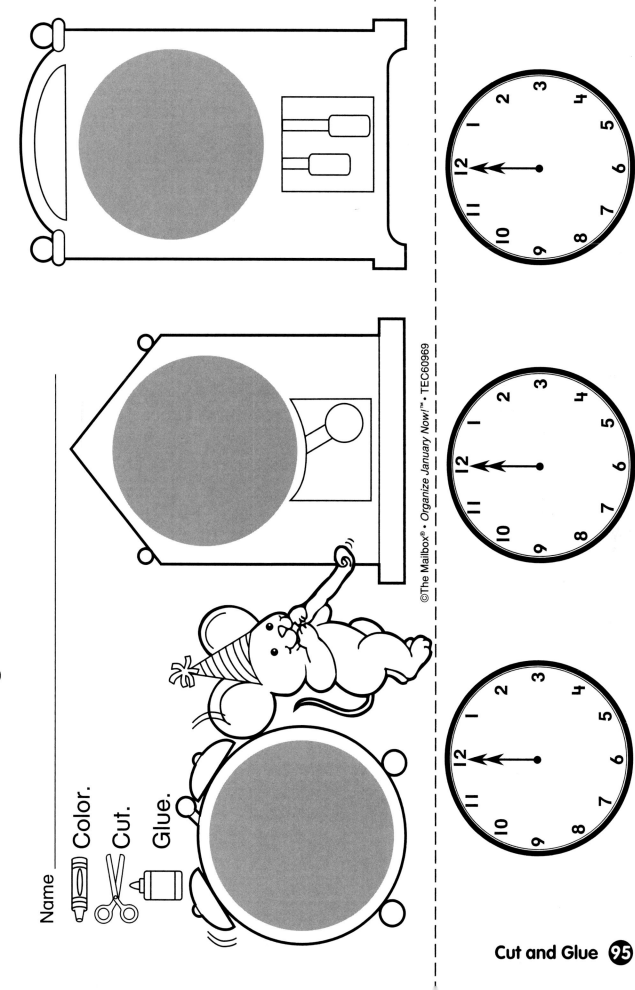

Name _____

Color.

Cut.

Glue.

Penguin Party

Name _____

🖍 Color.

✂️ Cut.

🗜 Glue.

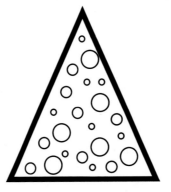
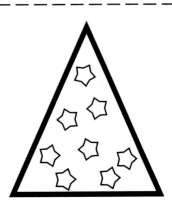